de Machines

Using Levers

Wendy Sadler

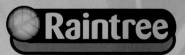

Chicago, Illinois

For information address the publisher:
Raintree, 100 N. LaSalle, Suite 1200, Chicago, IL 60602

Printed and bound in China by South China Printing
Company

09 08 07 06 05
10 9 8 7 6 5 4 3 2 1

Library of Congress Cataloging-in-Publication Data:
Cataloging-in-Publication Data is on file at the Library of
Congress.

ISBN 1-4109-1442-9 (lib. binding), 1-4109-1449-6 (Pbk.)

Acknowledgments
The publishers would like to thank the following for
permission to reproduce photographs:
Alamy Images (Comstock Images) p. **14**; Alamy Images
(Joe Sohm) p. **22**; Alamy Images (Michael Bojang) p. **20**;
Alamy Images (Robert Harding Picture Library) p. **16**;
Corbis p. **29**; Corbis (Jim Cummins Studio Inc) p. **23**;
Corbis (John & Lisa Merrill) p. **5**; Corbis (Pete Saloutos)
p. **26**; Getty Images (NBAE) p. **21**; Harcourt Education
Ltd (Tudor Photography) pp. **4**, **6–13**, **15**, **17**, **18**, **19**,
24, **25**, **27**.

Cover photograph of scissors reproduced with permission
of Corbis (George B. Diebold)

Every effort has been made to contact copyright holders of
any material reproduced in this book. Any omissions will
be rectified in subsequent printings if notice is given to the
publishers.

Disclaimer:
All the Internet addresses (URLs) given in this book were
valid at the time of going to press. However, due to the
dynamic nature of the Internet, some addresses may have
changed, or sites may have changed or ceased to exist since
publication. While the author and Publishers regret any
inconvenience this may cause readers, no responsibility
for any such changes can be accepted by either the author
or the Publishers.

Contents

Any words appearing in the text in bold, **like this,** are explained in the glossary.

Machines That Use Levers

Levers can be found all around you. You may even be able to see some from where you are sitting right now! A lever is a **simple machine.** It can also be part of many other machines. Simple machines can help us to do lots of different things.

A hammer can be used as a lever to pull a nail out of a piece of wood.

The blades of a windmill are big levers. Wind pushes against the ends of the blades and makes them turn.

Levers everywhere!

A bicycle, a piano, and a windmill all use levers to help them work correctly. Without levers, none of these machines would be able to do its job. Even the first computer used more than a thousand levers. Levers are very simple, but very important.

What Is a Lever?

A lever is a **stiff** bar or stick that moves around a point that does not move called a **fulcrum** or **pivot.** Levers are most often used to help us lift heavy things. Using a lever means we do not have to push or pull so hard to move an object. The push or pull that we use is called the **force.**

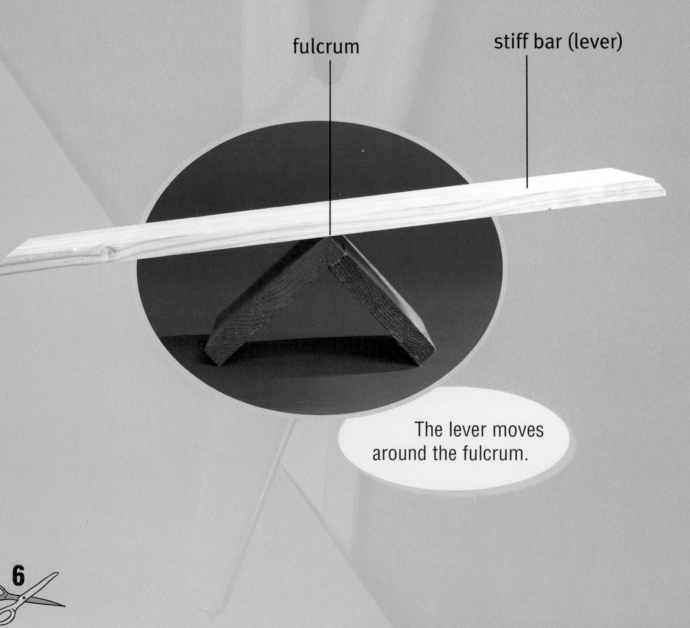

fulcrum

stiff bar (lever)

The lever moves around the fulcrum.

When you use a lever, there are two forces in action. The **effort force** is the force you use to lift or move the lever. The **resulting force** is the force that moves or lifts the object. The object you are trying to move or lift is called the **load.**

resulting force

effort force

fulcrum

load

What would happen without . . . ?

Opening this can would be difficult without a lever. You would need to get your fingers under the lid and then pull very hard upward.

7

What Is a First-Class Lever?

In a first-class lever, the **fulcrum** is between the **load** and the **effort force.** You push down on one end of the lever. This push is the effort force. At the other end, the lever moves upward and lifts the load.

The load is the **weight** of the thing you are trying to lift or move. You could also say that the load is the **force** you need to move something.

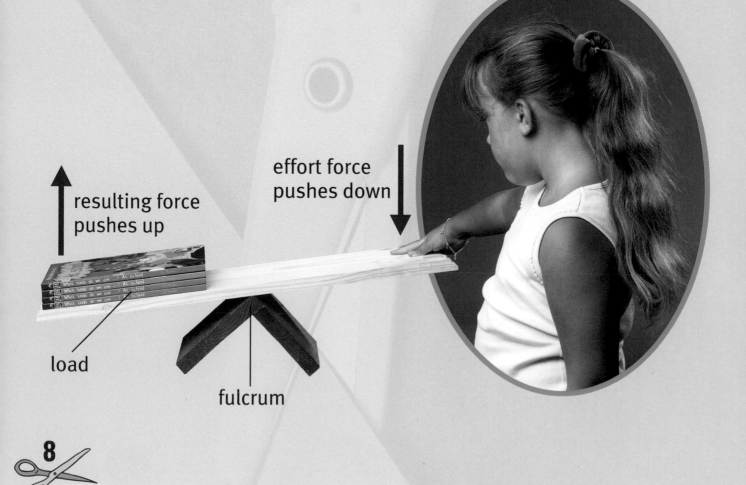

resulting force pushes up

effort force pushes down

load

fulcrum

If you move the fulcrum closer to the load, you can lift a weight using much less effort force. The distance you need to move the lever is bigger, but the effort force you need is less.

effort force

resulting force

Moving the fulcrum closer to the load means you need to push the lever down farther, but the load is much easier to lift.

Did you know . . . ?

Anything can be lifted with a lever if it is long enough. If you had a lever that was long enough, you could lift an elephant with just one hand!

9

Balancing Levers

fulcrum

bar (lever)

Scales use levers to weigh things. When the bar is level, you know that the weights on each side are the same. The scales will balance.

Not all first-class levers are used for lifting things. If the **fulcrum** is in the middle of the lever, it can be used to balance things. To balance something, there must be the same **weight** on both sides. With this type of lever, the bar is level when the **forces** on each side of the fulcrum are the same.

A set of scales is like a seesaw. Have you tried playing on a seesaw with someone who is the same weight as you? If you both sit still, the seesaw does not move upward or downward. The bar stays level because you both weigh the same. This means the forces are the same on each end of the lever.

If you play on a seesaw with someone who is heavier than you, it does not balance. This is because the forces are different.

If your friend is about the same weight as you, then the seesaw will balance.

First-Class Levers Together

The metal tab on a drink can is a first-class lever. The **fulcrum** is where the metal tab is joined to the can. The **load** is the metal shape that needs to be pushed down to leave a drinking hole in the can. This lever helps you to open the can without too much **effort force.**

effort force
pulls here

resulting force
pushes down here

lever

load

fulcrum

The metal tab is a lever that acts as as simple machine to help open the can.

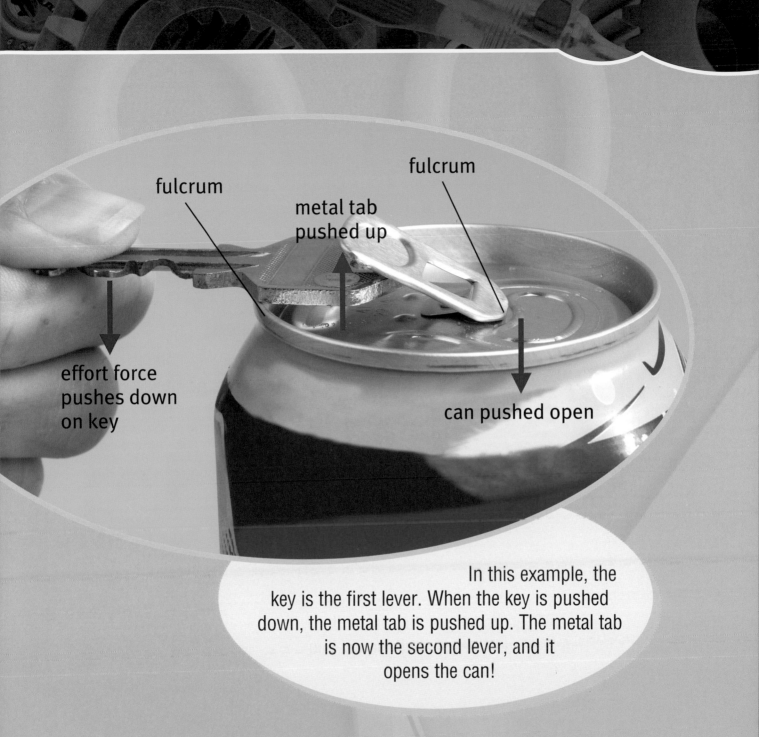

fulcrum

fulcrum

metal tab
pushed up

effort force
pushes down
on key

can pushed open

In this example, the
key is the first lever. When the key is pushed
down, the metal tab is pushed up. The metal tab
is now the second lever, and it
opens the can!

You may use a key or a coin to help you lift the metal tab
on a can. This is using two levers together. It means you
use even less effort force to open the can. A machine
that uses two or more **simple machines** together like
this is called a **compound machine.**

Cutting with Levers

When you cut paper with a pair of scissors, you are using two first-class levers. Each blade of the scissors is a lever. The two levers work together around one **fulcrum.** The fulcrum is where the two blades of the scissors are joined together. The fulcrum is between the **load** and the **effort force,** so these levers are first-class levers.

fulcrum

lever one

lever two

Both levers in a pair of scissors use the same fulcrum.

When the handles of scissors are apart, the blades are apart. You put an effort force on the handles by pushing them together. The paper is the load that you need to push through. The blades push against the load. The effort force from both blades together cuts the paper.

When you close the handle of a pair of scissors, you put in an effort force. The **resulting force** pushes the blades through the paper to cut it.

effort force

resulting force

What would happen without . . . ?

Without scissors, we would need to use one blade or a knife to cut paper. This could be very dangerous and not very neat!

What Is a Second-Class Lever?

A second-class lever carries the **load** between the **fulcrum** and the **effort force.** A wheelbarrow is an example of a second-class lever. When you lift the handles of a wheelbarrow, you also lift the load. You lift the handles farther than you lift the load, but it takes less effort than it would to pick the load up in your hands.

Without a wheelbarrow, it would take a lot of hard work to move heavy loads over long distances.

load

effort
force

wheelbarrow
moves forward

fulcrum

A door is a **compound machine** that uses two second-class levers. The fulcrum is where the **hinges** are. The load is the **weight** of the door. You put effort force on the edge of the door when you push or pull it open.

The handle is another second-class lever. The fulcrum of this lever is where the handle turns. The load is the weight of the handle.

fulcrum

handle

effort force

The handle on a door is a second-class lever that pulls the door catch in, so the door can open.

Levers in Humans!

Your foot is an example of a second-class lever. When you stand on tiptoe, the **joint** at the bottom of each toe is the **fulcrum.** Your **weight** is the **load.** This pushes down on the middle of your foot. The **muscles** in your leg give the **effort force** that lifts your heel. When these muscles tighten, your whole body is pulled upward.

effort force

load

heel

toes

resulting force

fulcrum

When you stand on tiptoe, the load is the weight of your body. Muscles work the lever inside your foot to pull your heel off the ground.

Other joints in your body act like levers, too. In your arms, your elbows work as fulcrums when you lift things up with your hands.

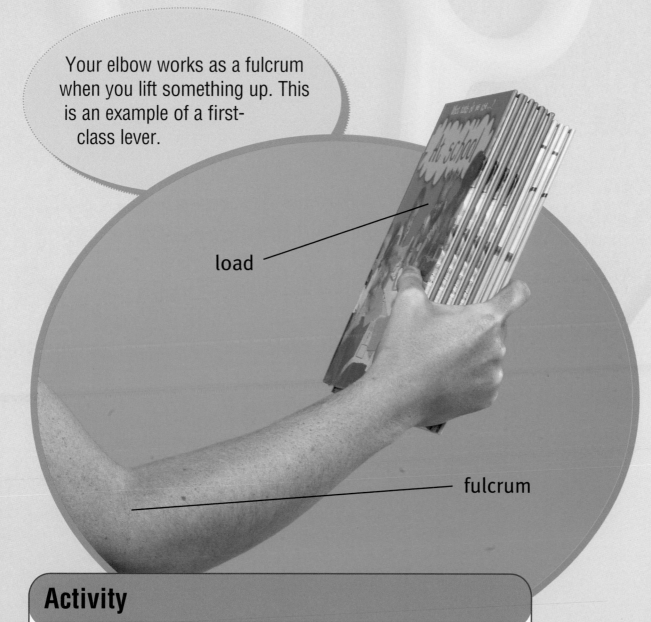

Your elbow works as a fulcrum when you lift something up. This is an example of a first-class lever.

load

fulcrum

Activity

You can become a second-class lever by standing on tiptoe. Can you feel your muscles tighten as they work the levers in your body?

What Is a Third-Class Lever?

In a third-class lever, the **fulcrum** is at one end of the lever. The **effort force** is between the fulcrum and the **load.** You use a large effort force over a small distance to move the load a large distance.

The paddle of this canoe is a third-class lever. The bar of the paddle is moved a small distance to make the load move a long way.

effort force

fulcrum

A fishing rod is a third-class lever. You use your wrist or elbow as the fulcrum. The fish on the end of the rod is the load. You have to put an effort force on the rod with your hand to lift the load up.

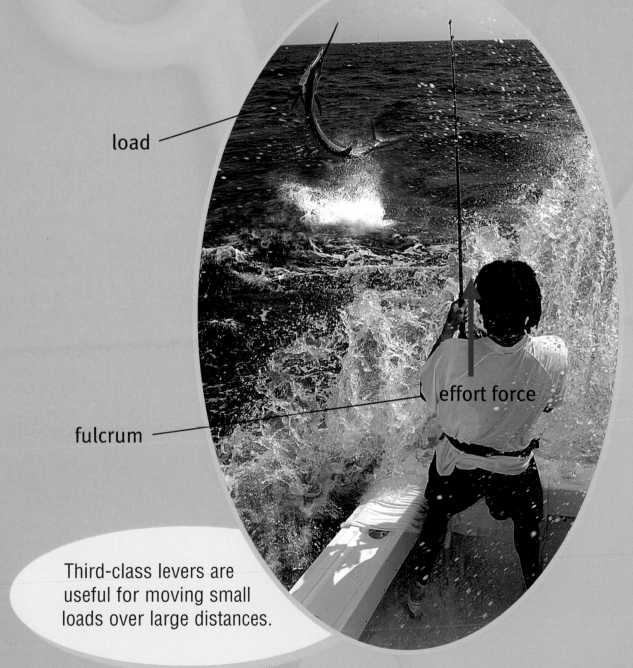

load

effort force

fulcrum

Third-class levers are useful for moving small loads over large distances.

Levers in Sports

Many sports use third-class levers. A baseball bat is a third-class lever. It is used to make the ball travel a large distance. The elbow acts as a **fulcrum** and the hands and arms give the **effort force.**

The bat is the **load** you need to move. When the ball hits the bat, it moves because the bat is moving. The ball moves from the end of the bat in the same direction as the effort force (your hands and arms) pushes the bat.

load

effort force

fulcrum

Other sports, for example tennis and badminton, also use third-class levers. Can you think of any other sports that use levers?

In tennis, the racket is a third-class lever that you use to help move the ball over the net.

What would happen without . . . ?

If we had to use our hands on their own to hit a tennis ball, we would not be able to hit it very far. It would probably hurt a lot, too!

Levers in the Garden

A shovel is a **simple machine** that can be used as two different kinds of lever. When you use your foot as the **fulcrum,** the shovel is a first-class lever. Your hand pushes down with the **effort force,** which covers a large distance. The other end of the shovel moves a small distance in the opposite direction, but with a big **force.**

effort force

fulcrum

resulting force

When you use your shovel to lift soil or plants, your body and the shovel together become a third-class lever. Your elbow now becomes the fulcrum. You use an effort force with your hand at the end of the shovel. The **load** is lifted in the same direction as your hand, but it moves a larger distance.

When you lift soil with a shovel, your elbow becomes the fulcrum. The effort force comes from your arm as it lifts the soil up.

effort force

load

fulcrum

Levers Working Together

A bicycle uses many levers together and lots of other **simple machines,** too. Pedals are second-class levers that help your legs turn the wheels. Handlebars are a first-class lever. Your hands turn them to make them become the **effort force** and the **load.** When you turn right, you pull with your right hand and push with your left.

handlebars

pedals

One of the **fulcrums** on a bicycle is in the middle of the handlebars.

small effort
force

A small squeeze of the brake lever on a bicycle can stop the entire load of the bicycle plus the **weight** of you on it!

Brakes are also first-class levers. The small **force** from your hands to squeeze the brake lever becomes a big force on the brake cable.

What would happen without . . . ?

Without levers in your brakes, you would have to pull on the brake cable very hard to make your bicycle slow down. This would hurt your hands and could be very dangerous.

Levers in Musical Instruments

A piano has hundreds of levers. The piano keys are first-class levers that you press down on at one end with your fingers. The other end of the key moves upward and pushes a second lever inside the piano. A stick attached to this lever pulls the end of another lever. A hammer is then pushed forward to hit the strings and make a sound.

When you push down on a piano key, you trigger a number of levers that are joined to a small hammer. The hammer hits a string that creates a musical note.

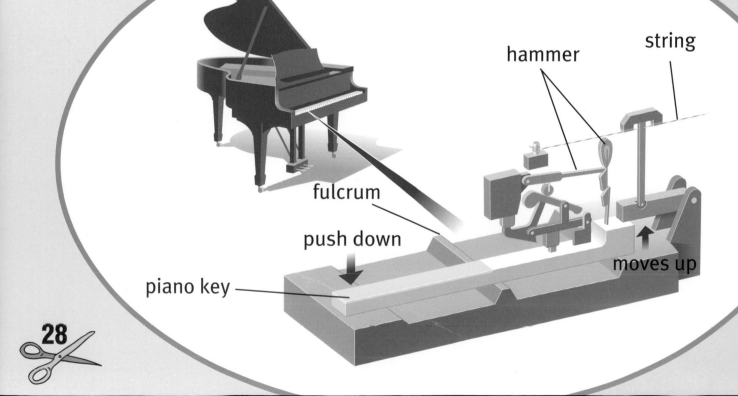

hammer

string

fulcrum

push down

moves up

piano key

The keys on a saxophone are also levers. They are second-class levers. The **fulcrum** is where the key joins the saxophone. When you push the keys, you move the lever so that it closes a hole in the instrument. The keys also have springs that push the lever back as soon as you let go.

fulcrum

A saxophone uses a lot of **simple machines.**

Find Out for Yourself

You can find out about levers by talking to your teacher or parents. Think about the **simple machines** you use every day. How do you think they work? Your local library will have books and information about this. You will find the answers to many of your questions in this book, but you can also use other books and the Internet.

Books to read

Glover, David. *What Do Levers Do?* Chicago, Ill.: Heinemann Library, 2001.

Tiner, John Hudson. *Levers*. North Mankato, Minn.: Smart Apple Media, 2002.

Using the Internet

Explore the Internet to find out more about levers. Try using a search engine such as www.yahooligans.com or www.internet4kids.com, and type in keywords such as "lever," "**fulcrum**," and "**effort force**."

Glossary

compound machine machine that uses two or more simple machines

effort force push or pull that you put into a lever to move or lift something

force push or pull used to move or lift something

fulcrum part of a lever that does not move. The bar or stick moves around it. It is also called a pivot.

hinge piece of metal that holds a door to the wall and lets it swing open and shut

joint something that connects two things together

load weight or object that a lever moves, balances, or pushes through

muscles parts inside the body that help us to move

pivot part of a lever that does not move. The bar or stick moves around it. It is also called a fulcrum.

resulting force push or pull you get out of a lever that moves or lifts something

simple machine something that can change the effort force (push or pull you provide) needed to move something or change the direction it moves

stiff something that does not bend easily

weight how heavy something is

Index